Terrific Teeth

by Janelle Cherrington

capstone
classroom

Look in a mirror and smile. What do you see? Teeth! Teeth come in many shapes and sizes. Why do we need teeth?

Teeth help us eat our food. This woman bites into a big peach. She uses her sharp teeth. These teeth are made to bite.

She squashes and chews the peach. She uses her side teeth. Side teeth are wide and flat. These teeth are made to chew.

Animals also need teeth to help them eat food. These front teeth are small and sharp. They help the squirrel split open hard nuts and seeds.

These teeth are wide and flat. They help the horse crush grass and hay.

Look out! These teeth are long and very sharp. They help the tiger bite into and rip apart meat.

Which teeth can eat meat? Which teeth can eat grass? How can you tell?

Essential Vocabulary

Phonics Words Introduced

crush, eat, flat, front, grass, meat, need(s), peach, see, seeds, she, small, smile, split, squashes, squirrel, teeth, these, we

Vocabulary Words

bite(s), chew(s), eat, food, front, sharp, smile, teeth

Sight Words

a, also, and, are, big, can, come, do, eat, help, her, how, in, into, long, look, made, many, need, open, our, out, see, she, the, them, these, they, this, to, us, use(s), very, we, what, which, why, you

PHONICS CONNECTIONS

People and animals need to eat food to stay healthy and alive. In order to eat, we need our teeth. In **Terrific Teeth** you will practice your phonics skills while learning about different kinds of teeth and why they are so important to people and animals.

capstone® classroom

www.capstoneclassroom.com

ISBN 978-1-62521-996-1